ORIENTAL COOKERY
for JUNIORS and BEGINNERS

by Kay Shimizu

ALMARK PUBLISHING CO., LTD., London

Dedicated with love

• Especially to niece Arden, nephew Stuart and son Glenn who shared my adventures and proved that junior cooks can both cook and eat exceedingly well!

• To special friend Flip who finds my left-overs fantastic. Bless him.

All rights reserved throughout the world. This book, or parts thereof, may not be reproduced in any form without permission of the publishers except for short quotations in critical essays and reviews.

All world-wide rights reserved under Universal Copyright Law
Copyright © 1973 by Kay Shimizu in Japan
Drawings by Minoru Tsushima

First edition 1973

First published by Shufunotomo Co., Ltd.
This edition by ALMARK PUBLISHING CO., LTD.
49 Malden Way, KT3 6EA, Surrey, England

Printed in Japan

Contents

Introduction	4
Asian Cooking Hints	5
What is Asian Cookery?	5
What Makes It So Unusual?	5
When You Cook......	6
Preparation of Ingredients	7
A Word of Caution About Ingredients	8
Utensils	9
Successful Menus and Pitfalls	10
Basic Asian Cooking Methods	11
Chinese Dishes	12
Japanese Dishes	34
Southeast Asian Dishes	56
Desserts and Potpourri	63
A Beginner's Asian Glossary	69
Index	71

Introduction

New waves wash ashore in our lives daily. Among them—exciting, tantalizing food flavor influences of the exotic—sometimes mysterious—Asian countries. These yummy recipes have been home-tested in America with easily available supermarket ingredients by many adventurous junior and beginner cooks from the enthusiastic students in my California cooking classes to inquisitive children interested in cookery. They all agree "creating a dish and getting to eat it is FUN—especially an Asian creation." They have discovered there is no mysterious "secret" to Asian cooking! And it adds such zest to dull diets. Besides you learn by eating which makes a wonderful excuse!

Confucius said, "How pleasant it is to repeat constantly what we are learning. You will soon be a master!" So trust me—easy does it. We all make mistakes but nothing succeeds like success!

Read and study my book first before you try to cook. This practical book is not only for beginners. Experienced gourmet cooks can benefit too. It is an introduction to a very extensive and a very intriguing international cuisine field. My previous book, ASIAN FLAVORS (Exposition Press, Jericho, New York), is a general basic text written in light conversational style and I suggest you seek it out for advancing your knowledge.

Relax and revel in your cooking adventure. Then join the feasting with your happy guests proudly and joyfully. Be content and gloat over the compliments as they fly...... "Great food!", "Where did you learn to cook?", "What restaurant did you order these scrumptious foods?"

Sharing a festive meal cheerfully together is one of the greatest ways to extend our circle of universal friendship and warm hospitality. May you eat better and enjoy it even more!

Kay Shimizu
Saratoga, California

A small start can become a great ending ...Old proverb

Asian Cooking Hints

What Is Asian Cookery?   What Makes It So Unusual?

- Wonderful mouth-watering aroma.
- Most of the time—very low calories.
- Beautiful natural fresh colors.
- Asian flavorings and spices make for exciting taste pleasures.
- Many dishes can be combined with Western-style favorites. Be daring! Be original!
- In all Asian countries rice is the staff of life and served at all family meals in place of bread. In some areas noodles are a standard substitute.
- Meat stretches and feeds more persons.
- Distinctive variety at every meal—a change from the monotonous meat and potato routine.
- "The Whole Earth" approach and ecology is not new in the Asian countries. It has been a necessity for them.
- Delectable shapes and textures.
- Exceedingly nutritious.
- Aesthetic arrangement of foods.
- Foods crispy, barely-cooked, tender-crunchy. Almost underdone!
- Diagonal cutting makes dish look especially Oriental.
- Uniformity of shape and size results in fast cooking. Vegetables, like humans, want identity.
- Many ingredients are already on your shelves to make foods taste Asian!
- Nothing is ever wasted. The Chinese, rich or poor, are known for their frugal use of every edible ingredient of land and sea. A most notable trait! We should follow suit.

Eating two-thirds vegetables and one-third meat results in good health...Confucius

ASIAN COOKING HINTS

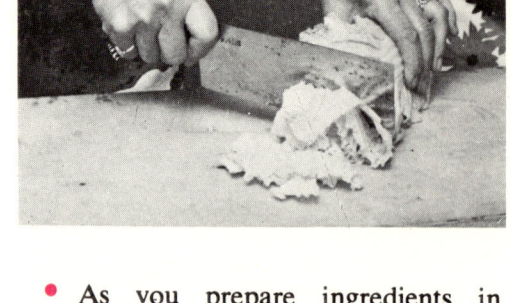

When You Cook......

- Be alert.
- Read recipes carefully first and follow exactly.
- Make sure everything is available before you begin.
- Take your time and cook with TLC—tender loving care.
- Get necessary ingredients and utensils out on your work area.
- All standard measurements are level.
- If ingredient is unfamiliar check the glossary section.
- As you prepare ingredients in advance line them up on a large tray—in neat stacks with sauce or gravy in a bowl also on same tray. Otherwise, what a disappointment to forget something and discover too late—wrong flavorings in wrong dish!
- Serve confidently and DEVOUR!
- Clean up kitchen mess and leave everything orderly.
- Result: You will be the happiest gourmet cook of exciting Asian foods. Practice makes perfect. Stay with it.

- Thousands of my students have learned already to cook Asian-style. You can too.
- Additional hint: Occasionally, go to an outstanding authentic Asian restaurant to taste what is professionally prepared. You will become even more confident than ever! You may eventually become better than the restaurant chef!

ASIAN COOKING HINTS

Preparation of Ingredients

You can do your cutting ahead and the actual cooking time is fast! No knives are served at an Asian meal so certain preparation fundamentals are very important in Asian cookery. And, your final dish will be more attractive. It is considered proper manners, however, to lift a piece of meat, for example, take a bite and replace it on your dish. Aren't you lucky how practical all this is?

- **Grate:** Scrape on a grater.
- **Mince:** Very finely chopped.
- **Shred or Sliver:** Cut like match sticks.
- **Dice:** Cut into 1/8–1/4 inch squares or whatever size is required.
- **Diagonal cut:** More surface is exposed for speed in cooking. Makes your cooking appear more Asian-like. One rarely sees American stew with diagonally cut vegetables—but it might be a good idea and an improvement.
- **Chunks:** Vegetable is rolled while you cut resulting in chunks with 1–2 inch sides.

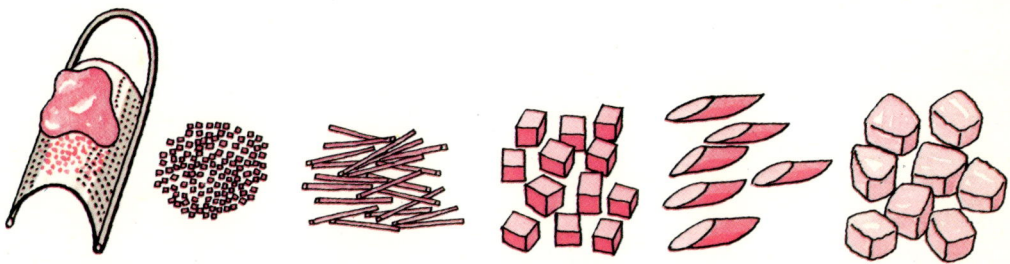

ASIAN COOKING HINTS

A Word Of Caution About Ingredients

• Please, no olive oil in Asian cooking. A limited amount of dairy products used on occasion but generally not.

• Many of the ingredients are the same all over the world. It is the flavorings and the method of cookery that make the same basic foods so special—so different—so good! So eat well!

• Some ingredients may be difficult to find away from the larger cities and strange to the Western eyes and nose! But availability of these foodstuffs is getting more universal so keep looking and ask your store clerks.

• Undercooking is the key rule in Asian cooking. This results in crunchy, natural vitamin-rich good flavors in your dishes. Examples are broccoli stir-fried takes only 3–4 minutes. Bean sprouts are only heated through and so it goes. It is the preparation of getting ready to cook that will take time. Plan and allow for it.

• When the recipe reads pork, chicken, etc. it means the raw state unless it specifies cooked.

• Sherry and MSG appear in some recipes. You can leave them out of my recipes without disastrous results. A pinch of sugar is a good substitute for MSG.

• Soy used in these recipes is all-purpose Japanese type. This way it is good for both cooking and table use. If Chinese cooking soy is used in the Chinese recipes use ⅓ less than called for since it is saltier. Do not use it for the Japanese dishes. I DO NOT recommend American-style soy sauce for authentic Asian flavor.

• A few exotic Oriental ingredients will have to be purchased but once bought you will find they stretch for many recipes. Your costs won't skyrocket with careful planning. But do not be mistaken that Asian cooking will be "cheap." It is not!

ASIAN COOKING HINTS

Utensils

● No special tools or utensils required although nice to have. A heavy skillet or Dutch oven will do.

● **A heavy rolled-steel 14 inch size Chinese wok** (like a large salad bowl-shaped pan) with supporting ring and special spatula are very good for all purposes—if you wish to get authentic.

● The Chinese cleaver and Japanese knives are indispensible but again not absolutely essential.

● A special steamer set is nice but you can devise your own like this:

Cut ends off of a flat tuna fish can.   Put in pot.   Fill water to just below level of can rim.   Bring to boiling.   Place your heatproof platter balanced on top of this can.   Cover pot.

● Kitchen tongs will help in cooking if you do not know how to use chopsticks.

● A rubber spatula with a wooden handle is a wonderful tool for stirring and cooking.   Few people use it this way but how fantastic.   Try it!

● I am a firm believer in using the best of each country's utensils, tools and recipes blending them interchangeably.   Be adaptable and flexible!

ASIAN COOKING HINTS

Successful Menus and Pitfalls

● Asian menus are far from monotonous—so do not plan all fried dishes, all pork entrees and so on.   Select with care and ease in your preparation.

● As beginners do not attempt to make a full assortment at first.   Incorporate these enticing Asian dishes which will generally serve 4 average appetites along with familiar Western foods.   For example: pork saté, rice, tossed green salad and jello.   They can be shared by more persons if several other dishes are included in the Asian manner.

● Don't fall in love with only one recipe.   It may be fast and simple and your favorite—but try to vary your menu and attempt others.   They will soon become just as easy.   Variety is the spice of life.

● Left-over Asian foods—the second day—despite the loss of fresh first-day crunchiness will still be fantastic.   Be sure to refrigerate.   Some of my devoted students even eat cold won tons, chow mein, etc. for great breakfasts.   And, why not?   All nutritious!

Learning without thought is labor lost...Confucius

ASIAN COOKING HINTS

Basic Asian Cooking Methods

Deep Frying: 2–3 inches vegetable oil is heated in a deep pot to about 350° F. Test with batter or cube of bread for correct browning temperature. Food must be completely immersed in hot oil to brown nicely.

Barbecuing: or Hibachi: Food grilled over prepared charcoal fire.   Doing it outside is ideal since smoke is dispersed.

Broiling: Preheat broiler of oven and foods are grilled on rack.

Steaming: Steam is very hot and takes only a short time to cook most foods— 15–30 minutes.   Constant swirl of steam cooks food.   Be sure you have plenty of hot water and replace as necessary.   Natural flavors are well preserved this way.

Stir-Frying: or Toss-Frying: Typically Chinese-style and similar to tossing a salad.   Keep tossing throughout cooking period.   You will get strong wrists this way!   Use very hot heat and a little oil.

Roasting: Baking with oven heat.

Chinese Dishes

......*Chinese dishes use a multitude of ingredients, spices and condiments with fantastic flavor results. Nicely cut and prepared with their main stress on "that special delectable flavor!"*

Fried Rice

Serves 4

Top of stove

A perennial favorite and a good way to use left-over rice or meat. Or, make rice early in the day "on purpose" and store in refrigerator so it gets cold and hard.

CHINESE DISHES

Ingredients:
1 Tablespoon oil
1½ cups cold cooked pork, chicken or ham, chopped into pea-size or slivered
1 small onion, chopped like peas
1 rib celery, chopped like peas
4 cups cold cooked rice (Chinese-style Texas Patna is ideal for this recipe)
2 eggs, slightly beaten
1 Tablespoon soy sauce
dash of MSG (optional)
dashes of salt and pepper to taste

How to prepare:
1. Heat skillet on high heat. Add oil and slosh around. Toss-fry meat, onion and celery about 2 minutes on medium heat until vegetables are transparent looking.
2. Keep toss-frying so ingredients will not burn.
3. Add cold rice. Break up the chunks so dry grains will separate. Keep up your toss-frying.
4. Heat ingredients thoroughly. Add the eggs. Stir well. Cook 1 more minute. Add rest of ingredients. Mix well. Taste to adjust seasonings.
5. Serve with extra soy sauce and perhaps some tomato catsup—if you like it that way.

Scarlet Shrimps

Top of stove

This is a winner for easy cooking and flavor!

Serves 2 as entree but 4 as a side dish

CHINESE DISHES

Ingredients:
1 pound large size shrimps
1 clove garlic, minced
a few gratings of fresh ginger
1 Tablespoon oil
2 Tablespoons hoisin sauce
2 teaspoons soy sauce
1 teaspoon sherry
dashes of salt and MSG (optional)
1 Tablespoon green onion, chopped

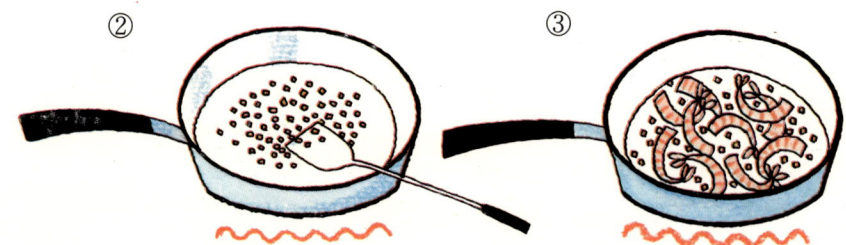

How to prepare:
1. Clean and devein shrimps. Leave shells on. Cut through back but not all the way. This will allow shrimps to curl nicely as they cook.
2. Heat pan on high heat. Add oil and slosh it around. Add garlic and ginger. Toss-fry ½ minute.
3. Add shrimps and toss-fry for about 3 minutes until slightly pinkish. Then add hoisin, soy sauce, sherry, salt and MSG. Toss-fry until shrimps are cooked about 3 minutes more.
4. Just before removing from pan mix in chopped green onions.
5. This is especially good as appetizers. Be sure not to eat the shells. Remove them between the teeth and tongue in Chinese manner—if you can, that is—or do it with your fingers!

Chinese Steak

Serves 4

Broiler or
  Barbecue

Like a "London Broil" and very quick to cook once meat has been soaked.

CHINESE DISHES

Ingredients:
1½ pound flank steak, left whole and not tenderized

Marinade:
1 clove garlic, minced
1 teaspoon fresh ginger, grated
½ onion, chopped
1 teaspoon oil
dashes salt, pepper and MSG (optional)
1 Tablespoon brown sugar or 1 Tablespoon honey
3 Tablespoons soy sauce
1 Tablespoon sherry

How to prepare:
1. Soak steak in marinade 4 hours or overnight.   Occasionally turn over.
2. Preheat broiler. Broil quickly 10–15 minutes altogether. Turning meat over once.   Do not overbroil.
3. Slice diagonally across grain to serve.   Should be slightly pinkish and very juicy.

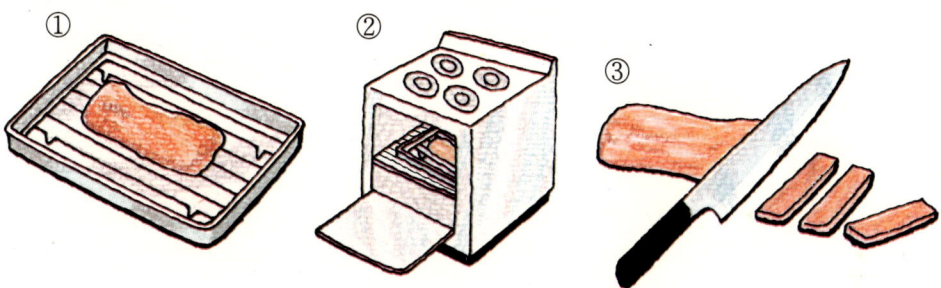

Fresh Egg Noodles in Soup

Serves 4

Top of stove

So quick and easy.   Particularly nice for a late snack.

CHINESE DISHES

Ingredients:
1 pound fresh thin Chinese-style egg noodles (soft kind) or substitute fresh Italian taglarini from delicatessen
2 cans commercially prepared chicken soup broth equal to 4 cups
¼ teaspoon fresh ginger, grated
a few drops sesame oil
½ teaspoon soy sauce
½ teaspoon salt, if necessary
MSG (optional)
green onions, chopped
2 hard boiled eggs, halved
a few slices of boiled ham, cut like matchsticks

How to prepare:

1. Boil plenty of water in a large pot and cook fresh noodles about 3–5 minutes. Do not overcook. Keep firm al dente. Drain. Run cold water through so starch will be washed off. Drain.
2. Heat soup. Add ginger, sesame oil, soy sauce, salt and MSG.
3. Warm cooked noodles by pouring hot water over them. Place in large individual bowls.
4. Pour hot broth over noodles. Garnish with chopped green onions, half of egg and slivers of ham. A little soy sauce can be added at the table.

Crispy Fried Fish

Serves 4

Top of stove

Frozen turbot fillets work wonders in Chinese cookery. Use this good and inexpensive fish wherever flounder is suggested. The flavor of turbot remains excellent even after 6 months in freezer storage.

CHINESE DISHES

Ingredients:
1 pound Greenland turbot fillets, cut 1 by 2 by 2 inch pieces

Marinade:
3 Tablespoons soy sauce
¼ to ½ teaspoon 5-spices
1 Tablespoon sherry
2 teaspoons sugar
1 teaspoon fresh ginger, grated
dash of MSG (optional)
Chinese parsley, chopped (optional, but good)
cornstarch for coating
toasted white sesame seeds for garnish
chopped green onions for garnish

How to prepare:

1. Marinate fish in soy sauce, 5-spices, sherry, sugar, ginger, MSG and Chinese parsley for 1 hour.   Drain.
2. Put some cornstarch on a plate and coat fish pieces carefully on all sides.
3. Heat oil 2 or 3 inches deep in heavy pan to 350°F. Deep-fry until brown and crisp—about 5 minutes.   Drain on paper towels.
4. Heat a small heavy fry pan and toast sesame seeds.   Refer to glossary for method.
5. Sprinkle sesame seeds and chopped green onions over fish.

Simple Fire Pot

Serves 4

Top of table
Electric skillet

A very practical way to prepare a festive type of dish. You do the work of getting the ingredients ready but your diners actually do the cooking at the table. This is my favorite for a cold winter night. A leisurely way to dine...and can take two or three hours at the table. Or a speedy 30 minutes if you dash through the process!

Ingredients:

8 cups chicken broth
a bunch of green onions, sliced in 1 inch pieces
⅛ inch slice of fresh ginger
1 pound raw shrimps, shelled, deveined and slit in half
½ pound pork, sliced very thin, ⅛ by ¾ by 2 inches
1 large piece chicken breast, sliced very thin
about 4 cups leafy green vegetables such as lettuce, Chinese cabbage (nappa), spinach, watercress, etc.
assorted dips as listed in the recipe

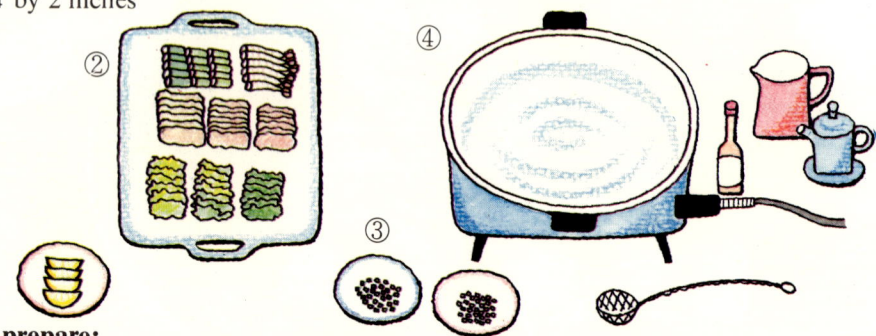

How to prepare:

1. Put broth, green onions and ginger into an electric skillet. Do not heat yet.
2. Prepare all other ingredients as directed. Place artisically on a platter.
3. Fill sauce dishes with dips and place on table. These can be any kind you desire such as soy, hoisin sauce, tomato catsup, mustard paste, tabasco sauce, chopped green onions, chopped peanuts, lemon wedges, sesame oil and so on. Try your own ideas. Anything goes!
4. Now—heat broth at table. A little salt, sherry and MSG can be added for flavor if you like.
5. When broth bubbles everyone adds some meat and vegetables from the plat-

ter either holding with chopsticks or a special net spoon. As these cook only about one minute each time—dip in a blend of sauces and eat while hot with bowls of steamed rice.

6. Keep adding more meat and vegetables as each person desires more. Serve remaining broth as a soup adding more water if it has become too concentrated. Rice or noodles and dashes of the desired sauces are added as flavorings. It is all a fantastic blending of good flavors!

Vegetables Stir-Fried

Serves 4

Top of stove

Cooked this simple quick method and served with all-American juicy hamburgers, rice and salad you have the makings of a nourishing balanced meal with a difference!

CHINESE DISHES

Ingredients:
2 or 3 pounds vegetables such as Chinese cabbage (nappa), string beans,
   mushrooms, green peppers, bok choy, etc. (all one kind or a combination)
1 Tablespoon oil
1 teaspoon salt, more or less to taste
⅛ inch slice of fresh ginger ⎫
1 clove garlic, crushed   ⎬ spear on toothpick
½ teaspoon MSG
dash of water
dashes sugar, pepper and soy sauce

How to prepare:
1. Prepare vegetables in uniform 1-1½ inch lengths or chunks as the case may be.
2. Heat skillet on high heat.   Add oil.   Slosh it around.   Add ginger and garlic. Toss-fry for ½ minute.
3. Add vegetables, sprinkle water and seasonings. Keep toss-frying over high heat.   Cook for 2–3 minutes.
4. Taste.   Adjust seasonings to your liking.   Should be still very crunchy.   Remove garlic and ginger.   Serve with mustard paste and soy sauce.

Meat Balls with Sweet and Sour Sauce

Serves 4

Top of stove

Another way to make our favorite hamburger standby a family satisfying flavor.

Ingredients:

1½ pounds very lean ground beef, sirloin or round
1 egg
6 Tablespoons cornstarch
1 onion, minced
⅛ teaspoon black pepper
1½ teaspoons salt
1 clove garlic, minced
a few gratings of fresh ginger

CHINESE DISHES

How to prepare:

1. Blend all ingredients well in bowl. Dampen your hands. Form meat into 1 inch diameter balls. If too sticky, add more cornstarch.

2. Heat skillet over medium heat. Add 1 Tablespoon oil. Slosh it around. Put in meat balls. Turn occasionally to brown well. Will take about 7–10 minutes on medium heat. If there is any excess oil, drain off.

3. While meat is cooking make the sauce:

Sweet and Sour Sauce:
   Ingredients:
   2 teaspoons soy sauce
   2 Tablespoons cornstarch
   8 Tablespoons sugar
   6 Tablespoons cider vinegar
   4 Tablespoons tomato catsup
   1 cup pineapple juice or water
      or a combination of both
   dashes of MSG and salt

4. Blend carefully in saucepan. Cook over medium low heat. Stir constantly until thickened and translucent in appearance.

5. Add the following and keep stirring while the ingredients heat through about 5 minutes.
   1 drained can of sweetened pineapple
      chunks (either large or small can)
   1 or 2 green peppers, cut into chunks
      with 2 by 2 inch sides
   1 onion, cut like peppers in chunks
      and pieces separated

6. Just before serving blend in the meat balls and pour everything over a bed of thinly sliced lettuce leaves.

7. You can make it fancy and sprinkle chopped nuts such as peanuts, almonds and a few chopped green onions over the top of the sauce covered meat balls.

Delicate Eggs

Serves 4

Top of stove

An interesting method of egg cookery—by steam.   Pleasant smooth texture.

28

CHINESE DISHES

Ingredients:
6 eggs
½ cup finely chopped chicken, turkey, shrimp or pork (raw or cooked)
1 Tablespoon oil
1½ teaspoons salt
¾ teaspoon sugar
1 Tablespoon sherry
2 cups chicken stock
dash MSG (optional)
2 stalks green onion, chopped for garnish

How to prepare:
1. Start water boiling in a deep pot ready for steaming.
2. Beat eggs slightly. Add rest of ingredients except green onions and blend well in large heat-proof ceramic or glass pyrex bowl.
3. Place carefully on rack in steamer. Cover with pan lid. Steam at medium heat for about 20 minutes. Test center with knife blade and if it comes out clean it is done. Garnish with chopped green onions.
4. Sprinkle a little soy sauce on top just before serving. This is eaten hot.

Sweet Roast Pork

Serves 4

Oven or barbecue

Succulent irresistible morsels of real Asian flavor! Be the first in your group to know how to make this. Makes a terrific sandwich, too!

CHINESE DISHES

Ingredients:
1½ pounds lean pork butt or tenderloin, sliced in 1½ by ¾ by 4 inch long strips

Marinade:
4 Tablespoons brown sugar
1 teaspoon salt
2 Tablespoons honey (clover is nice)
1 Tablespoon sherry
2 Tablespoons Chinese parsley (do not substitute regular parsley—omit if you do not have Chinese parsley)
a few gratings of fresh ginger
1 clove garlic, minced
2 teaspoons soy sauce
¼ teaspoon Chinese 5-spices or substitute allspice
1 teaspoon red food coloring or ¼ teaspoon char siu salt (saltpeter)
dash MSG (optional)

How to prepare:
1. Soak meat in marinade for 1 day in refrigerator.   Turn occasionally.
2. Heat oven ten minutes in advance to 350°F.
3. Place on rack over a pan of hot water.   The broiler pan set is excellent for this.   Put meat on rack.   Roast 45 minutes.   Turn once.
4. Watch carefully so meat will not get charred.   Baste with any left-over sauce in bowl.   Slice meat into ⅛ inch slices.   Serve hot or cold.

Chicken with Assorted Vegetables

Serves 4

Top of stove

A standby Chinese "toss-fry" entree that goes well with hot rice or noodles. A speedy dish once you master the basic cooking method.

CHINESE DISHES

Ingredients:
2 cups chicken meat, shredded (use breasts or thighs)
1 clove garlic, minced ⎫
½ teaspoon fresh ginger, grated ⎬ placed on top of meat
1 medium onion, sliced ⅛ inch thick
3 ribs celery, sliced diagonally ⅛ inch thick
1 cup water chestnuts, sliced ⅛ inch thick
1 cup fresh edible pod peas or substitute fresh green string beans, sliced diagonally
½ pound fresh bean sprouts, washed and drained
1 cup fresh mushrooms, sliced ⅛ inch thick

Gravy:
2 Tablespoons soy sauce   1 Tablespoon sherry
1 teaspoon salt   1 teaspoon sugar
1½ Tablespoons cornstarch   1 teaspoon sesame oil
1 teaspoon MSG   1 cup water or stock

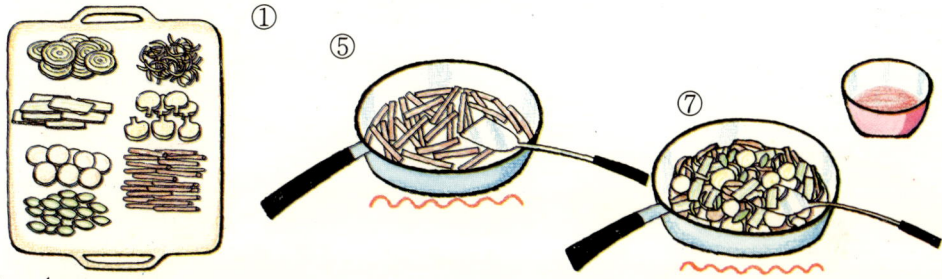

How to prepare:
1. Prepare all raw ingredients carefully.   Stack them in neat piles on a large tray.
2. Mix and stir gravy ingredients in a small bowl.   Place on large tray along with prepared ingredients.
3. Heat skillet on high heat.   Add 1 Tablespoon oil.   Slosh all over pan bottom.
4. Add onion, celery and water chestnuts.   Stir-fry until heated through about 3 minutes.   Add edible pod peas, bean sprouts and mushrooms. Toss and stir-fry another 1 minute to heat completely.   Remove from pan.
5. Clean skillet.   Reheat and add 1 Tablespoon oil.   Slosh around pan.   Add meat with the garlic and ginger at the bottom directly into the hot oiled pan. Keep toss-frying until meat is whitish about 3 minutes.
6. Add well-mixed gravy ingredients and cook until translucent.   Keep tossing.
7. Blend in pre-cooked vegetables.   Toss-fry again until heated through about 2 more minutes.   Serve with soy sauce, mustard dip and rice of course.

Japanese Dishes

......*Japanese dishes emphasize pleasure in small quantities of food beautifully cut and prepared—then arranged like an artistic picture for viewing eyes and for your discerning taste to savor.*

Fried Crispy Pork

Serves 4

Deep-fried

This pork cutlet (tonkatsu) looks very Western. It is a safe bet for someone who is leery of strange foreign flavors.   Left-overs make good sandwiches.

JAPANESE DISHES

Ingredients:

A ⎧ 1 pound lean pork steaks, ¼ inch thick cut from loin
　　 2 Tablespoons soy sauce
　　 2 Tablespoons sugar
　　 a few gratings of fresh ginger
　　 1 clove garlic, finely minced
　　 dash of salt
　　 ⎩ dash of MSG (optional)

handful of flour on a plate
1 egg, beaten, and diluted with ½ cup cold water
bread crumbs (or Japanese panko)
vegetable oil for deep-frying
a few leaves of cabbage for garnish

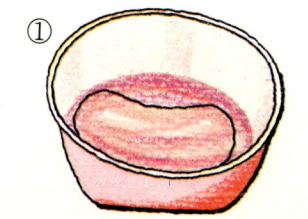

How to prepare:

1. Soak A in a bowl for 1 hour.
2. Coat steak with some flour. Then into egg mixture and finally dip into the loose crumbs.
3. Let stand on a plate for 30 minutes for crumbs to adhere better.
4. Heat oil 2 inches deep to 350°F. in a heavy pan.
5. Fry carefully and do not brown too quickly since pork must be well done. Will take about 5 minutes on each side.
6. Drain on paper towels. Serve with very thinly shredded cabbage strips. Serve with soy sauce, tomato catsup or tonkatsu sauce. This store-bought special tonkatsu sauce is like steak sauce and great with hamburgers, steaks and even hot dogs!

35

Glazed Beef Teriyaki

Serves 4

*Broiler or
   Hibachi*

Everyone's favorite at Asian bazaars—now you know how to make it and can have your own bazaar!   No great mystery.

JAPANESE DISHES

Ingredients:
2 pounds lean beef such as flank, cross rib, sirloin, etc. sliced ⅛ by 1 by 3
a few gratings of fresh ginger
1 clove garlic, minced
½ onion, chopped fine
5 Tablespoons soy sauce
4 Tablespoons sugar
4 Tablespoons sherry (optional)
dash MSG (optional)

How to prepare:
1. String meat stretched out on wooden skewers. Do not crush meat pieces tightly together.
2. Mix all other ingredients well in a flat pan. Add meat on skewers. Turn over occasionally for flavors to penetrate. This should marinate 2 hours or longer for best flavor.
3. Heat broiler in oven and broil 2 inches from heat for 3–5 minutes or less. No need to turn meat over usually. Do not overcook since it will dry out the meat.
4. A charcoal fire is the ideal method. Crusty, brown and so succulent! The soaking of the sticks along with the meat prevents burning wood while broiling!

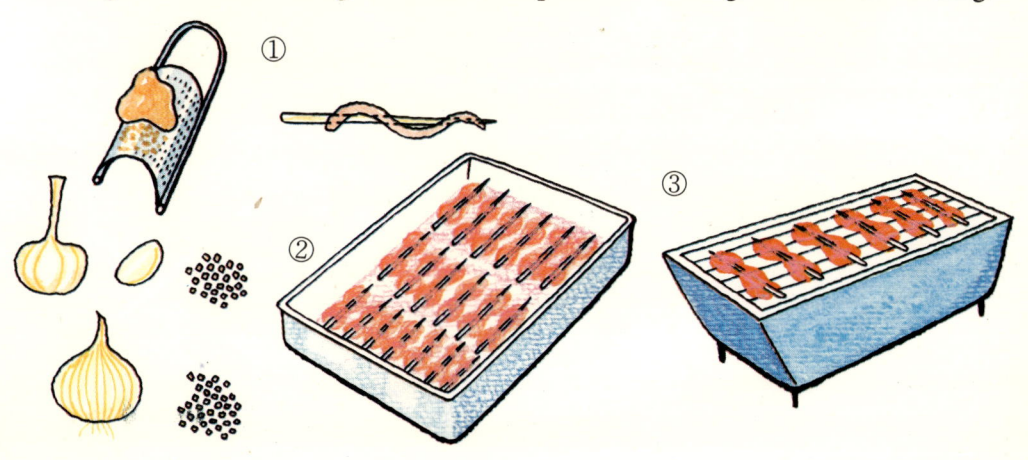

Barbecued Shrimps

Grill or broiler

Serves 4

So speedy to fix—so succulent—leaving the shells on will help to retain good color and good flavors. Also, it prevents people from eating them up too FAST!

JAPANESE DISHES

Ingredients:
1 pound raw shrimps (the largest size available), deveined through shells leaving shells and tails intact
dashes of salt and MSG (optional)
2 Tablespoons soy sauce
1 Tablespoon sherry
1 teaspoon sugar
1 teaspoon sesame seeds
1 Tablespoon green onions, chopped for garnish
wedges of lemon for garnish

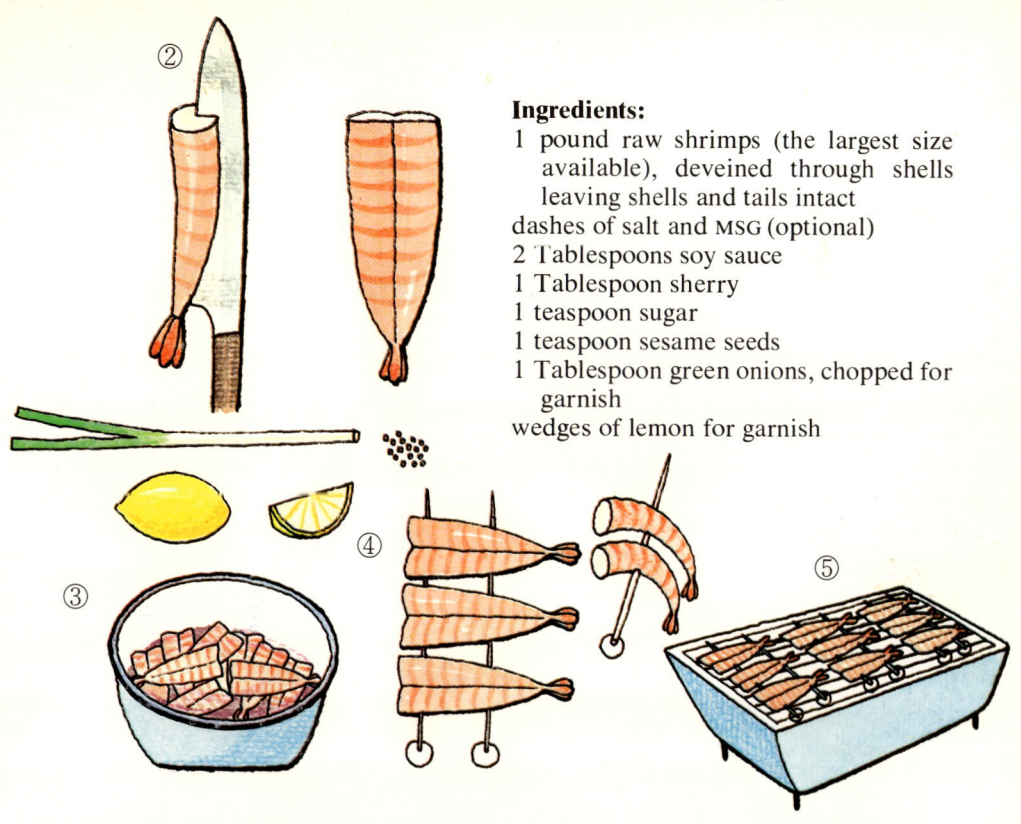

How to prepare:

1. Prepare your hot coals in the outdoor brazier or preheat your broiler.
2. Split shrimps carefully at back with a sharp knife but do not cut all the way through.   This is called butterfly-cut.
3. Sprinkle salt, MSG, soy sauce, sherry, sugar and sesame seeds on prepared shrimps.   Soak for 15 minutes.   Mix occasionally.
4. Spear the shrimps on long stainless steel skewers, if available. Otherwise substitute shorter wooden ones.
5. When your coals are a very nice gray ash grill shrimps 3–5 minutes turning as necessary.   Do not overcook.   Remove to a platter with a garnish of chopped green onions and wedges of lemon.

Sweet Omelet

Serves 4

Oven

This is a very easy oven adaptation of a favorite Japanese egg recipe which is customarily made on top of the stove in a fry pan.

JAPANESE DISHES

Ingredients:
6 large eggs
1 Tablespoon sugar
6 Tablespoons Japanese soup (dashi) or chicken broth
½ teaspoon salt
1 Tablespoon sherry
dash MSG

How to prepare:

1. Preheat oven to 275°–300°F.
2. Blend the above ingredients well in a bowl.
3. Oil a 9 by 9 by 1 inch baking pan with a paper towel. Be sure you do not make it too oily.
4. Pour above mixture in pan. Place in hot oven. Do not disturb. Bake slowly for 15 minutes until surface is firm to the touch and set. Do not worry if it forms and sets bubbles.
5. Remove from oven and allow to cool. Loosen all edges carefully with a spatula. Cut into 1½ inch squares.
6. Lift carefully with a small spatula onto a platter. Try to make it attractive. Garnish with parsley. Serve at room temperature. Excellent in place of the usual boiled eggs for a picnic.

Pork with Bean Cake

Serves 4

Top of stove

Here is a very simple method of preparing delicate custard-like soy bean cake. This tofu sponges up the intriguing flavors.

JAPANESE DISHES

Ingredients:
1 pound pork, sliced 1 by ¾ by ⅛ inch pieces
1 teaspoon fresh ginger, grated
1 bean cake (tofu)—large Japanese fresh firm type, cut into 1 inch squares
2 medium size onions, sliced in half, then in ¼ inch slices

Gravy:
4 Tablespoons soy sauce (Japanese shoyu)
3 Tablespoons sugar
1 Tablespoon water
1 Tablespoon sherry (optional)
dash MSG (optional)

How to prepare:
1. Prepare meat, ginger, tofu and onions.   Get gravy ingredients measured out in a small cup.
2. Heat skillet until hot.   Add 1 Tablespoon oil.   Add the pork and ginger. Cook until whitish for 5 minutes over medium heat.
3. Add the balance of ingredients.   Keep ingredients separated as much as possible.   This will result in a more attractive final dish.
4. Simmer for 5 minutes over medium heat.   Take a small pancake turner and carefully turn over the bean cake, meat and onions to allow flavors to penetrate during this cooking time.
5. Remove to platter cautiously and garnish with a few green onions, chopped, if desired.
6. Variation: A celery rib could be sliced diagonally and added at the same time as the onions.   This dish is not to be toss-fried.   This is a typical Japanese one-pot cooking style...and ingredients are allowed to simmer.

43

Chicken Sukiyaki

Serves 4

Top of table
  Electric skillet

Pronounced s'kiyaki but call it what you like.   You'll be understood.

Ingredients:

- 2 pounds raw boneless chicken meat, sliced 1 by 2 by ½ inch
- 1 can shirataki (yam noodles) or substitute dried bean threads (sai fun). Soak bean threads in hot water for 15 minutes then cut into 2 inch lengths.
- 1 bunch green onions, sliced diagonally 2 inches long
- 1 bulb onion, halved and sliced ½ inch thick
- 2 cups fresh mushrooms, sliced ½ inch thick
- 1 small can bamboo shoots, sliced ¼ inch thick
- 1 soybean cake (tofu), cut in 1 by ¾ by ½ inch pieces
- 2 cups spinach or other greens such as Chinese cabbage or outer leaves of lettuce, cut 1 inch lengths

Sauce:
- ½ cup soy sauce
- 4 Tablespoons sugar
- ½ cup broth or water
- ½ teaspoon MSG
- ¼ cup sherry

How to prepare:

1. Arrange all raw ingredients in a nice pattern on a large platter. Try to make it look attractive. Mix the sauce ingredients in a small pitcher ready for use.
2. Heat electric skillet on high heat. When hot add a little vegetable oil and coat surface of skillet.
3. Add portions of meat slices and vegetables in neat groupings in the pan. Pour part of sauce over everything. Allow to simmer. There should be enough liquid so ingredients will not stick to bottom of pan. Turn over if necessary in a careful manner for flavor to penetrate better. This is Japanese cooking and not a toss-fried hash! Cook only 3–5 minutes.
4. Help yourself from skillet as food is cooked. Be sure to have hot steaming bowls of Japanese-style rice to go with sukiyaki.
5. Add more raw ingredients and repeat process. Adjust seasoning if you like it more sweet or more salty. Sauce ingredients may be increased if desired.
6. Dipping the hot morsels into raw beaten egg as you eat is the "real" way but certainly not everyone eats it this way! Some persons just cannot get used to the slippery egg on the surface of the food. But try it sometime. I think it is superb that way.

①

Elegant Spinach

Top of stove

Spinach prepared this method will make even spinach "haters" like it.

Serves 4

JAPANESE DISHES

Ingredients:

1 large bunch fresh spinach, clean, remove wilted or bruised portions, cut off just below pink root.   Leave leaves attached to root area.

A ⎰ 2 Tablespoons soy sauce
   ⎪ 1 Tablespoon dashi or chicken broth
   ⎨ dashes of sugar
   ⎩ dashes of MSG (optional)

2 Tablespoons toasted sesame seeds, black or white, see glossary for toasting instructions

How to prepare:

1. Boil spinach in lots of boiling water for 2–3 minutes. Turn once. Becomes a bright green color. Drain. Run under cold water to stop cooking process.
2. Squeeze excess water out and line up spinach in a neat row. See how nicely the leaves stay in place since the root was left intact.
3. Cut into 1½ inch lengths. Grasp a batch of strands and squeeze out the water that still remains.
4. Arrange upright on a colorful plate and mix A ingredients in a bowl. Pour over spinach. Garnish with toasted sesame seeds. Observe, the sauce trickles down the spinach leaves.

47

Nigiri-Rice

Serves 4 or more

No cooking after rice is cooked

The polite way for ladies to call these rice balls would be "o-nigiri." These are great getaways. Pack up a tempting picnic lunch and go! Usually formed into shape with wet hands but for beginners follow these simple instructions—unless you have asbestos hands! Teriyaki goes super with these.

JAPANESE DISHES

Ingredients:
3 cups raw Japanese rice freshly cooked and fluffed up ready for use
salt
1 Tablespoon toasted sesame seeds, black or white

How to prepare:
1. Wet an 8 by 8 by 2 inch baking pan with water. Drip off excess but do not dry with towel.
2. Sprinkle lightly with salt. Pack hot rice into pan carefully. Very firmly compress the rice so it will be level with wet fingertips. Spread a foil over top and invert quickly on bread board.
3. Heat a heavy small skillet and toast sesame seeds. Refer to glossary for method.
4. Sprinkle surface of rice with toasted sesame seeds. Cut rice block carefully with a sharp wet knife into 1 by 2 inch rectangles. These can be eaten either hot or cold.

Oyako Donburi

Serves 4

Top of stove

A hearty quick "meal in one"—literally translated "parent and child (the chicken and egg) in a bowl." An easy lunch.

JAPANESE DISHES

Ingredients:
1 cup raw medium-grain Japanese-style rice cooked ready for serving hot
¾ pound chicken meat or use one large breast
2½ Tablespoons soy sauce
1 cup chicken broth
2 teaspoons sugar
½ teaspoon salt or more to taste
dash MSG (optional)
1 small can sliced mushrooms, drained or 2 or 3 medium-sized fresh mushrooms, sliced
½ package thawed frozen peas
2 green onions, sliced ¼ inch
3 eggs, slightly beaten together

How to prepare:
1. Slightly freeze chicken first to make it simpler to remove bone.
2. Cut into ½ inch cubes or slices.   Place in bowl and add soy.
3. Heat broth, add sugar, salt, MSG and chicken soaked in soy sauce. Stir carefully. Cook 3 minutes.
4. Add mushrooms, peas and green onions.   Cook 2 minutes more.
5. Blend 3 eggs in small bowl until mixed. Pour eggs into pan with other ingredients.   Cook 3 minutes carefully shaking pan by handle to distribute flavors. Eggs will be soft and coddled but set.
6. Place hot cooked rice ¾ full in large individual bowls (donburi) or use soup bowls.   Scoop the chicken-egg mixture over rice. A little sprinkle of dried flavored seaweed is often used for garnish in the center of the serving.

51

Turnip Surprise Pickles

Serves 4–6

No cooking

A delicious nibble and a taste surprise especially when you have always hated turnips before. In America turnips are not consumed as in years past. It will be a new discovery prepared like this.

JAPANESE DISHES

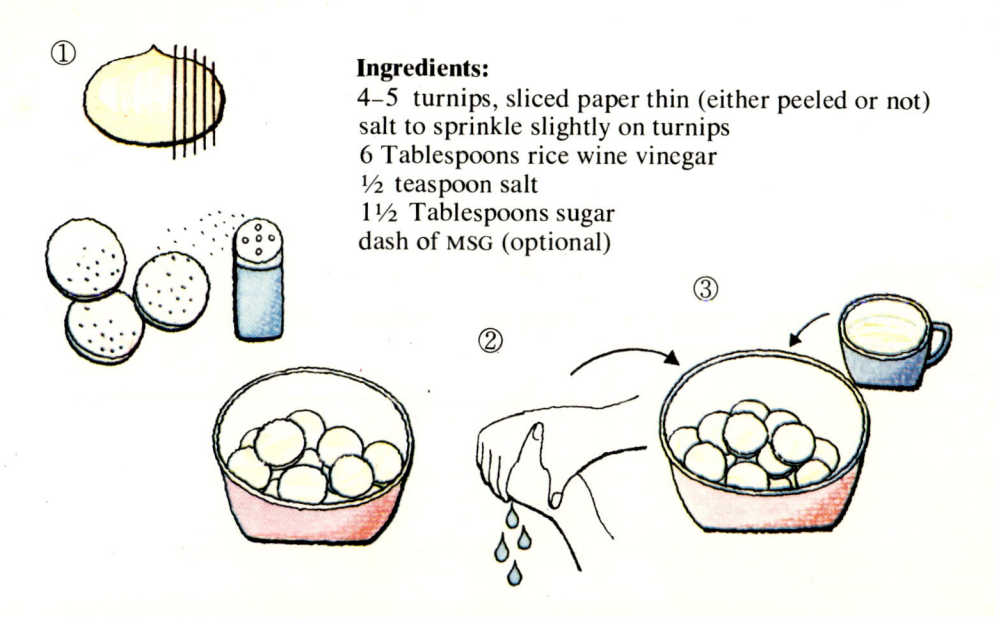

Ingredients:
4–5 turnips, sliced paper thin (either peeled or not)
salt to sprinkle slightly on turnips
6 Tablespoons rice wine vinegar
½ teaspoon salt
1½ Tablespoons sugar
dash of MSG (optional)

1. Put sliced turnips in bowl. Salt slightly and allow to rest until soft about 20 minutes.
2. Gently squeeze turnips dry with hands. Discard juices.
3. Sprinkle with 2 Tablespoons rice wine vinegar over the squeezed turnips. Massage the limp turnips a few times. Squeeze more liquid out again and discard the juices.
4. Mix well the remaining 4 Tablespoons rice wine vinegar, salt, sugar and MSG with the dry turnips in a bowl.
5. Let stand several hours mixing occasionally. Get some green leaves from your garden like bamboo and wash well. Spread on platter. Place seasoned turnips along with the leaves. Strips of fresh lemon rind can be used as garnish along with the turnips on the plate. Looks attractive.
6. Red food coloring can be used if you want a pinkish tint.

53

Quick and Easy Chicken with Vegetables

Serves 4

Top of stove

A one-pot meal when served with rice...like a stew...but faster to prepare!

JAPANESE DISHES

Ingredients:
1 pound chicken meat, cut into 1 inch chunks
4 Tablespoons soy sauce
3 Tablespoons sherry
2 Tablespoons sugar
dash of MSG (optional)
¼ cup dashi or chicken broth
1 teaspoon fresh ginger, grated
½ pound fresh string beans, cut diagonally 1 inch long
1 onion, cut in half, then in ¼ inch slices

How to prepare:
1. Place chicken, soy sauce, sherry, sugar, MSG, broth and ginger in deep pot.
2. Heat over high heat. As it comes to a boil lower heat to medium.
3. Grasp edges of pan and shake up and down occasionally with care to blend flavors.
4. Continue to simmer with a cover. After 10 minutes add string beans and cook 5 minutes or more. Add onions and shake again as above. Cook 2 more minutes. Adjust flavorings if you wish more sweetness.
5. Keep the vegetables crispy-tender. Do not overcook.
6. Serve with bowls of hot Japanese rice.

Southeast Asian Cooking

......*Filipino dishes are a delightful mixture of Chinese and Portuguese taste...so very flavorful. Malaysian, Indonesian and Vietnamese dishes have all been influenced very much by the Chinese although they use more curries, hot chilis, spices, pungent fish and shrimp sauces.*

Fantastic Chicken en Adobo (Filipino)

Serves 4

Top of stove

This magnificent tasting chicken almost "cooks itself!" And the aroma is irresistible. It can be made ahead of time very nicely.

SOUTHEAST ASIAN DISHES

Ingredients:
1 chicken fryer, about 3 pounds, cut up into serving pieces, remove any extra fat or heavy skin
5 Tablespoons cider vinegar
1 clove garlic, minced
¼ teaspoon pepper
1 bay leaf
dash of MSG (optional)
1½ teaspoons salt, more if desired
2 onions, cut in quarters
boiling water

How to prepare:
1. Put everything except the boiling water in a large bowl and allow to soak for 15 minutes.
2. Place in a large pot or wok.   Add enough boiling water to cover the chicken.
3. Simmer covered until the liquid disappears.   About 45 minutes.   Be patient. It will soon all evaporate.   The aroma at this point is marvelous!
4. If there is very little fat left in the pan from the chicken and not sufficient for frying add 2 Tablespoons of bland vegetable oil.
5. Continue to pan-fry on medium heat with the cover off until the chicken is slightly browned on both sides.   Check to make sure you do not burn the chicken. Serve on a large platter along with hot steamed rice.

57

Pork Saté (Indonesian)

Serves 4

Grill or barbecue

Firey hot—but delectable!   Real gourmet flavor.

SOUTHEAST ASIAN DISHES

Ingredients:
2 pounds lean pork, cut 1 inch thick, then into ½ inch cubes
1 onion, chopped fine
2 cloves garlic, minced
½ teaspoon ground coriander
1½ teaspoons salt
¼ teaspoon black pepper or more
dashes of cayenne pepper
3 Tablespoons lemon juice
2 Tablespoons brown sugar
4 Tablespoons soy sauce
1 Tablespoon vegetable oil

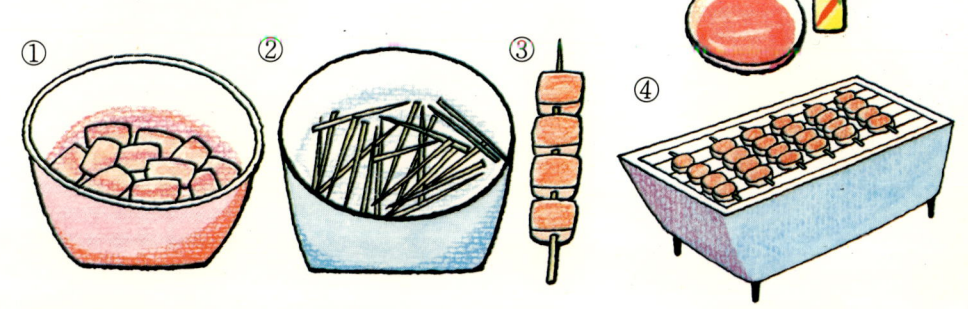

How to prepare:
1. Mix and soak above ingredients two hours at room temperature. Turn occasionally.
2. Soak about 24 wooden skewers in cold water to prevent burning later when you are barbecuing the meat.
3. Thread cubes onto wooden skewers.
4. Heat oven broiler or make hot coals in hibachi. Broil meat two inches away from heat. Brush a little vegetable oil on meat to keep moist. Turn occasionally. Grill 10–15 minutes until done. Cut a piece of meat to see that it is no longer pink inside. Pork must be well cooked.
5. Usually served with hot chili and Indonesian sweet soy condiment but this is probably "hot" enough for you already.

Golden Pilau with Chicken (Malaysian)

Serves 4

Top of stove

Very festive, brilliant and colorful rice and chicken combination. Definitely exotic!

SOUTHEAST ASIAN DISHES

Ingredients:

A {
1 fresh 3 pound chicken fryer, not cut up
one stalk green onion tied in a knot
2 cloves garlic, left whole
1 teaspoon salt
}

1½ cups raw long-grain rice
4 Tablespoons butter or use as much as 8 Tablespoons, if you desire
4 stalks green onions, chopped
1 onion, diced
2 cloves garlic, minced

a few gratings of fresh ginger

B {
1 teaspoon turmeric
1½ teaspoons salt
several dashes of pepper
MSG (optional)
¼ teaspoon chili powder or 1 fresh red hot chili pepper, slivered
1 teaspoon prepared curry powder
⅛ teaspoon ground coriander seeds
⅛ teaspoon ground cumin
}

1 carrot, cut like matchsticks for garnish

How to prepare:

1. Clean chicken well.   Remove extra chunks of yellow fat or heavy skin.
2. Simmer A in a large pot covering with hot water for 45 minutes.   Turn chicken over once during the simmering process.
3. Remove chicken.   Cool.   Remove bones but try to keep meat in large pieces.   Discard any very fatty sections of skin.
4. Strain broth.   Remove excess oil floating on top of broth.   There should be about 2½–3 cups broth in pan.   Cook raw rice in this broth.   Refer to Chinese-style rice cooking method in index.   When cooked, fluff up for use.
5. Melt butter in a skillet.   Fry 4 green onions, diced onions, minced garlic and ginger for 1 minute.   Add chicken, brown and crisp.   Season with all seasonings listed under B.
6. Stir into hot rice mixing carefully.   Taste.   Add more seasonings if desired.   Garnish with carrots.

SOUTHEAST ASIAN DISHES

Stormy Flavored Chicken (Vietnamese)

Serves 4

Top of stove

Familiar fried chicken with a firey, spicy difference that really bites back! Have a glass of water handy to stop that sting!

Ingredients:

- 2½ pound chicken fryer, cut-up into serving pieces
- 1 clove garlic, minced
- 2 Tablespoons oil
- 1 teaspoon salt
- ¼ teaspoon pepper
- MSG (optional)
- 1 teaspoon dried red chili flakes or many dashes of cayenne
- a small handful of peanuts without skins, chopped
- Chinese parsley and green onions, both chopped for garnish

How to prepare:

1. Heat pan over high heat. Add oil and slosh it around. Fry chicken and garlic until crispy brown about 15–20 minutes. Add salt, pepper and MSG.
2. Arrange chicken on platter. Garnish with red chili flakes, peanuts, Chinese parsley and green onions.

Desserts and Potpourri

......*Heavy sweet gooey desserts do not follow authentic Asian meals. If anything, fruits, gelatin concoctions or ices are excellent. But, if you like, go ahead and have chocolate cake! I do sometimes.*

Ginger Ice Cream

A very little ginger crystallized or preserved in honey is good when chopped up fine and added to softened vanilla ice cream or fruit for an Asian Westernized dessert. But again this is only if you and your guests like ginger. Garnish with a cherry.

DESSERTS AND POTPOURRI

Kōri

Serves as many as you plan for

No cooking

Recently an American touring Japan ordered curry, trying to give it what he felt was the regional pronunciation. The waitress to his surprise responded, "Do you wish lemon or strawberry?" He tried again, "No, I want kare." His original had sounded like kōri!

This is a very refreshing and a most popular Japanese snack—like an American "sno-cone." There are kōri stalls everywhere in Japan. This would be a most refreshing dessert for an Asian meal.

Ingredients:
ice cubes or chunks of ice
concentrated sweet fruit punch base or thawed frozen fruit juice concentrate

How to prepare:

1. Grate ice cubes as fine as possible with whatever ice crusher you have. If you do not have one, put ice in a small sturdy cloth bag. Go outside where you cannot damage anything and whack the bag with a hammer until finely crushed.
2. Place mounds of shaved ice in sherbet glasses. Pour the fruit flavored base over the ice. Lemon, strawberry, melon, green tea syrup and sweetened beans are favorites in Japan. Probably you will try a tropical fruit flavored base, orange or perhaps grape. Experiment.
3. There is a really nice imported Japanese icer that stands upright and makes very finely shaved ice. Wonderful for a gift for the kids and terribly handy for adults to borrow for their daiquiris!

DESSERTS AND POTPOURRI

Rice

Serves 4

Top of stove
    or
Electric cooker

The truly easiest way to cook rice is using an electric rice cooker (same proportions as top of stove cooking method) but since it is still not a common appliance in Western homes—here is the next best way. Asians do not use salt in preparing rice but add if you prefer.

Japanese-style Rice

Medium grain "Rose" rice type is gummier than the Chinese-style. Measure 2 cups raw rice and place in a strainer. Run under cold water and stir with fingers until water is clear. Wash well. Add 2 cups water. Cook on high heat in a heavy pan with lid. When water bubbles over reduce heat to very low. If using an electric stove place on another burner on low. Proceed to cook for 20 minutes more. Do not peek! Let it steam for 5 to 10 minutes more.
Loosely fluff up the kernels with a wet rice paddle or wooden spoon to serve.

Japanese-style Rice

Chinese-style Rice

Texas Patna long grain rice is drier and flakier than the Japanese type. Prepared the same as above except use the proportions of 2 cups raw rice to 2½ cups water. (This Chinese-style rice is the best rice type for making fried rice with all kernels flaky and separate. Be sure to use old left-over or "cooked early-on-purpose" rice. Not hot from the pan.)

DESSERTS AND POTPOURRI

How to Make A Good Pot of Tea

Japanese green tea and tea pot (Sino-Yaki)

    Tea is the main native drink in the Orient as opposed to coffee in Western countries. There are many varieties but the two common types easily available are green tea which looks pale straw color when brewed and black tea (oolong) which looks red when brewed. The Japanese favor green tea and the Chinese go more for oolong for family use.

    The ideal way to make tea is to warm the tea pot first with boiling water. Drain it then the leaves are added. Water that has just come to a boil is poured over the tea leaves and allowed to stand for about 2 or 3 minutes.

    For weak tea I find about 1 Tablespoon (1 tea bag) is enough for a 4 cup tea pot. Directions on the tea packages always tell you to use more. I think this is a promotion to sell more tea! Serve plain without cream, sugar or lemon for there is a special lightness and fragrance to tea. But if you like to put in cream or whatever go ahead.

DESSERTS AND POTPOURRI

Crunchy Soybean Nuts

Serves many

Oven

Amazing soybeans have proportionately more protein than many other sources like steak and eggs. This recipe makes a very healthy, energy packed snack.

Ingredients:
1 cup dry soybeans, wash well
2 teaspoons oil
salt or other seasonings

How to prepare:

1. Soak beans overnight in bowl with plenty of water.
2. Preheat oven to 350°F.
3. Drain and dry beans with paper towels.
4. Place oil on cookie sheet then the nuts. Shake well.
5. Roast 45 minutes. Stir occasionally. Sprinkle salt, garlic salt, grated Parmesan cheese or use some of the commercially prepared dry salad dressing or dip mixes. Here's a chance to really experiment with taste buds!

DESSERTS AND POTPOURRI

Garnish Tricks and Relishes

No cooking

To decorate your platter, your salads, your main dishes—or just to munch on—here are some selected fanciful ideas.

Carrot Flowers: Cut into ⅛ inch slices after you have made grooves all down the outer length of the carrot. Decorate center with a sliver of lemon peel.

Green Onion Sprays or Brushes: Slice white portion of the green onion stalk into 2½ inch lengths. Sliver tips with a sharp knife by cutting into the green onion on both ends about ¾ inches. Soak in ice water and the onion will "flower." These can be used for garnish but also can be used as brushes for applying sauce on meat and so on while you eat.

Tomato Flowers: Peel a regular good round shaped tomato carefully in one continuous strip. Rearrange peelings into a round red rose.

Radish Accordions: Select good shaped radishes and make slices part way down on one side of the radish. Soak in ice water and they will open up slightly to reveal the white flesh.

Beautiful Flowers
The easiest way to make shapes like flowers is to buy little Japanese ¾ to 2 inch stainless steel cutters shaped like flowers. Use carrots, daikon and other firm vegetables. Also one can use these same Oriental cutters for making miniature cookies and the larger cutters for making small appetizers from bread.

A Beginner's Asian Glossary

Bamboo shoots: Young tender shoots come in cans. Keep in refrigerator covered with water. Change water daily. Will keep about one week. Do not freeze since crunchy texture will be lost.

Bean Cake (tofu, dofu): Fresh soybean cake. Highly perishable. Keep covered with water in refrigerator.

Bean sprouts: Sprouted from mung beans. I especially recommend fresh ones when available. Do not overcook. Cook only about 1 minute or crunchiness will be lost. Fussy Asian cooks remove beans and roots but I never bother.

Bok choy: Swiss chard type of Chinese vegetable but not similar in taste—dark green leaves with ivory ribs. Cooked like Chinese cabbage (nappa).

Char siu salt: Chilean saltpeter available at Oriental butcher shops. This is different from drug store variety. It gives meat a brick red color throughout like corned beef. Substitute red food coloring if unavailable. Or omit from recipe.

Daikon: Japanese white long radish that looks like a carrot but larger. Substitute white icicle radish.

Dashi: Japanese seasoned soup base prepared from fish and seaweed for Japanese cooking. Please do not use for Chinese dishes. Usually I substitute chicken broth for Westerners. It is less "fishy" in flavor and has more appeal and more delicacy for uninitiated palates.

Dried mushrooms: Chinese and Japanese types used in these recipes. Flavor is different from European varieties. Soak in warm water for 15 minutes. Squeeze dry before use.

Garlic: A clove of garlic refers to one the size of your baby finger tip. To peel the very easy way: smash (no need to whack!) with slight pressure from flat side of cleaver blade. Dry outside skin will just fall off—almost! This method will leave you without pungent odors under your fingernails for days to come.

Five spices: A very aromatic blend of cinnamon, anise, fennel, cloves and Chinese mild pepper. Use sparingly. If unavailable make up your own fairly good substitute by mixing together 1 teaspoon powdered cinnamon, 1 teaspoon aniseed, 1 teaspoon thyme, 1 teaspoon powdered cloves and a dash of allspice. Some of my students love this zesty flavoring so much they use it for making cookies and other non-Asian delicacies.

Ginger: Fresh bulbous root. Do not substitute ground ginger spice or your Asian dishes will have a faint "gingerbread" flavor—better to omit if not available.

Hoisin sauce: Sweet vegetable sauce—dark brown color used as a condiment and for cooking much in the same manner that we use catsup. Try it brushed over your barbecue chicken. Transfer contents from can to a jar.

Monosodium glutamate: Abbreviated MSG. A flavor enhancer from natural organic sources. It has recently been proven that it is harmless in small minute quantities. A dash of sugar can be used as a substitute.

Mustard: Dry mustard powder mixed with warm water to a paste to be used as a dipping condiment usually with Chinese dishes. Dashes of oil, vinegar, soy and sugar can be added for a more flavorful dip. And this is HOT!

Nappa or celery cabbage: Chinese cabbage—not truly of the cabbage family. More like lettuce. Very mild flavor. Used either raw or cooked. Experiment adding to your regular green salads or cole slaw.

Oil: Use bland oil. Peanut oil is ideal but cottonseed, corn and safflower are quite satisfactory.

Rice wine vinegar: Very mild fragrant vinegar made from sweet glutinous rice. Looks like clear water. White distilled vinegar diluted with water could be substituted but the genuine article is unsurpassed for flavor in Asian dishes.

Sai fun: Bean threads made from mung beans. Other names are cellophane noodles, long rice, transparent vermicelli and silver threads. Soak in hot water 15 minutes to soften before use.

Sesame oil: Derived from sesame seeds. Very potent in fragrance. Use for flavoring foods such as vanilla is used for cakes. I do not recommend it for cooking use.

Sesame seeds: Two varieties—black and white. To toast use heavy pan heated over high heat. Add no oil. Add seeds. Shake vigorously until seeds jump. Do not burn.

Sherry wine: Use dry sherry for cooking although other white wines are quite satisfactory.

Snow peas: Fresh edible pod peas available in season. Frozen ones are expensive and get mushy upon cooking. I substitute thawed frozen regular peas or fresh string beans.

Soy sauce (shoyu or soya): All purpose Japanese light style used in this book for both table and for cooking.

Water chestnuts: Fresh or canned tubers with rough brown skin. When peeled—very pearly white inside. Crunchy sweet vegetable and retains crispiness despite cooking. Freezes well covered with water. Keeps in refrigerator for one week with frequent changes of water.

Wintermelon: Squash family but looks like a miniature watermelon. Dark green chalky outside skin. Pure white flesh and mild tasting. I have discovered you can substitute the white part of a regular watermelon and it works. No one will know! Try it sometime.

Even if you have many rice fields you can only eat one day's portion daily...Chinese

✳✳✳✳✳

And finally the end. But hopefully the beginning of many more culinary delights for you. The kids won't have to be told, "...and you can eat hot dogs!"...because many of them can now cook along with you new flavors themselves that they really like. In fact they may now be turning the tables and saying, "You can have hot dogs, Mom!"

Index

Barbecued Shrimps, 38

Chicken Sukiyaki, 44
Chicken with Assorted Vegetables, 32
Chinese Steak, 16
Crispy Fried Fish, 20
Crunchy Soybeans, 67

Delicate Eggs, 28

Elegant Spinach, 46

Fantastic Chicken en Adobo, 56
Fresh Egg Noodles in Soup, 18
Fried Crispy Pork, 34
Fried Rice, 12

Garnish Tricks, 68
Ginger Ice Cream, 63
Glazed Beef Teriyaki, 36
Golden Pilau with Chicken, 60

Kōri, 64

Meat Balls with Sweet and Sour Sauce, 26

Nigiri-Rice, 48

Oyako Donburi, 50

Porke Saté, 58
Pork with Bean Cake, 42

Quick and Easy Chicken with Vegetables, 54

Rice, 65

Scarlet Shrimps, 14
Simple Fire Pot, 22
Stormy Flavored Chicken, 62
Sweet Omelet, 40
Sweet Pork Roast, 30

Tea, 66
Turnip Surprise Pickles, 52

Vegetables Stir-Fried, 24

About the Author

Kay Shimizu is a Japanese American born in Oakland, California, who has been researching, experimenting, teaching and tasting exotic Asian foods for over 25 years. To help junior cooks world-wide—a beginner of 10 years or 60 young years—to prepare popular Asian foods the easy way has been a long time burning desire. Thousands have attended her Asian cooking classes which she teaches on the West Coast.
She has authored many books and is presently writing another on Asian cookery. Mrs. Shimizu is a student of Japanese culture, history and calligraphy and has many hobbies in the arts and crafts. Her engineer husband, Esau, and she live in Saratoga, California.